CHESS AND SPORT

STEVE BO KEELEY

ISBN-13: 978-1502808622

ISBN-10: 1502808625

This book was printed in the United States of America.

First Edition

1 2 3 4 5 6 7 8 9 10

Keeley, Steve Bo
Chess and Sport —1st ed.

Published by Service Press

Thanks to Dr. Bud Muehleisen for his story 'The Search for Bobby Fischer End on a Racquetball Court'.

To order additional copies of this book contact:
Amazon.com or bokeely@hotmail.com

DEDICATION

To my father who taught me chess over a funny book.

Introduction

Is chess a sport? Chess today is a recognized sport of the International Olympic Committee, and after deep analysis *The NY Times* (2009) answered 'Maybe, Maybe Not'. After a lifetime in sports, including professional racquets, my answer is that chess is the headquarters of sports.

This book describes the myriad applications of chess to sport, and in particular to my forte racquet sports, where I was six-time national paddleball champion, and the #2 ranked racquetball pro for many years. However, my better sports were judo, football and hiking.

My credentials in chess are the Junior Chess Champ of the Michigan farm community of Jackson, and the founder of various clubs and winner of many tournaments for which I carved the trophies, as I did a three-dimensional chess set at age ten.

This is how chess guided me into sports. I saw everyone on the court or field as pieces on the board. Anyone who wishes to learn how to play chess in sport may well become conversant in positions where the players are, were, and will be. Chess opens the eyes to a sequence of moves in sports, and to identify those action frames, lock on one, and alter the fate of play and championships.

All sports are sweaty chess.

Contents

Pieces in a Box

---*1*---

As a kid, our Idaho family home didn't get *The NY Times*, so my math-minded father one winter conjured a chessboard, set up little men like ants, and told me to move them as seemed logical by their stature. In one year I was beating him while reading funny books. He threw up his arms in disgust, and a week later Santa left *How to Win at Chess Openings* by Al Horowitz under a pine tree in the living room.

Having spent an alarmingly chunk of the next year at the solitaire chess board, my mother encouraged me out to sports, and I undertook them with an onerous chess mind, flicking baseball pitches onto a canvas bull's-eye and football passes into a swinging bushel basket.

In winter, it was chess again, but also taking a shovel and rubber ball to the nearest vertical wall to remove the snow and bounce, bounce the ball for hours in practicing what I didn't quite know. The correct assumption was that solutions to problems I didn't know yet would crystallize, just like on the chessboard. If a theory sleeted in a blizzard, I retreated down the basement steps to the furnace room to bounce a basketball around pieces of coal that were the defense, and practiced it.

Anyone who wishes to learn how to play chess in sport may well become conversant in positions where the players are, were and will be.

This is how chess guided me into sport, and especially racquet sports where I became a six-time national singles champion in paddleball and #2 ranked racquetball pro throughout the decade of the '70s.

Opening

2

Chess opened my eyes to a sequence of moves in sports, and to identify those action frames, lock on one, and alter the fate of play. I started the Charlevoix, Mi. junior high chess club and bought a small trophy from a pawn shop that still gathers dust in my desert trailer. Three years later, I won the Jackson, Mi. junior chess championship against a boy who had hair on his face. When the Parkside high school tennis coach, Dennis Kiley, kicked me off the team for using chess moves and unorthodox strokes to defeat the #2 seed for a position on the team, I punched the clock on sports until going to Michigan State University veterinary school.

There, between chicken science and feeling fat marbling in pig hams, I got my A__ kicked by a string of Mensa cross-trainers at the MSU chess club and turned energies to paddleball and racquetball.

Racquetball has been described as 'chess at 150 miles per hour' for good reason. A chess game like racquetball may be divided into three parts: The open, middle and end games. Throughout the match on board or on court there are also tactics, strategies, combinations, practice, coaches, tournaments, politics, analysis, clock, scorecard, match point, and aesthetics. Grand masters as and national sports champs are well-versed in all.

The rackets opening resembles chess on these points:

- Winning begins with the choice of serve by 'white' and the service return by 'black'.

- Success comes with control of the center of the board and court.

- The opening establishes the middle game that affects the end game.

- Study new opens in chess, and of serves and returns in rackets.

- A finite number of variations in the open in any event must be analyzed to improve.

- The *Oxford Companion to Chess* lists 1,327 named openings and variants that range from quiet positional play to quick mate. *The Complete book of Racquetball* (by the author) lists thirteen opens that vary from stalls to crack aces.

- The chess gambit of rackets is the early game set-up to test the opponent's backhand.

- Capture of the adverse King is the ultimate but not the first object of the game, and there are other objectives than scoring in the sports opening.

- Game pace is established in the open.

- A ceiling game or baseline play in tennis imitates

the Queen's gambit that clogs play to await an error by the opponent.

- The chess master and pro openings are studied by amateurs for quick progress

- White and the server are at an immediate advantage if they play aggressively.

- Black and the receiver should strive to equalize a strong opening until an error is made and then move to attack.

- Chess has the blitz and rackets the Big Game.

- A surprise chess opening or a trick serve - legal screen, Z-serve, moving service motion, Wong's toss to the lights, Cliff Swain's camouflage drive ace to either side, or my backhand wallpaper serve along the wall – may single handedly win a tournament.

- Dull openings that win for a player but put the gallery to sleep, such as the chess French Defense and racquetball Garbage Serve, impact politics and sponsors.

- The purpose of the opening is to create an arena where the opponent is less comfortable than you.

The open usually matches the player's personality and game style: Aggressive, defense, or wait with counters in prey. My favored King's Gambit blew open wild combinations with many pieces on the board to force concentrations. Likewise, in paddleball and racquetball, the drive serve fetches the most setups for a potent killshot... but so many drives from the service box wore me out, and I converted to use that opening only for a quick lead or the end *coup de grace.*

The Ruy Lopez got my attention on taking Spanish because it was aggressive like the language, and at nearly every move there are reasonable alternatives. Lopez, a Spanish Priest, advised, 'Sit your opponent with the sun in his eyes.' My ninth grade science teacher and chess mentor, 6'10'' John Veenstra of Charlevoix, Michigan, set up the pieces near the window each sunny afternoon after school at his boarding house with the ranks parallel to the pane of glass. Each of us sat drenched in equal light. I applied the Lopez variation and reflected sunlight off the face of my watch into his eyes during his moves. It scored a rare win, with an after game bellyache, and so I retreated from that sort of gamesmanship. Even at my racquetball peak in the Golden Era, in 1978, on reading that Russian Viktor Korchnoi had distracted Anatoly Karpov with mirrored sunglasses in hopes of a world championship, cheating put me in mind of the pane. Karpov, like me in racquetball, is widely considered the strongest player to have never become the world champion.

There was a fine line in early paddleball and racquetball opens between gamesmanship and violence. The pre-game handshake meant more when a 250lb college jock tried to stare you down while crunching the metacarpals. I stopped shaking hands with the big lugs until after handing them losses. The three McNamara brothers of Minnesota, Bernie, Bob and Pinkie, were a large hunk of the Minnesota Gopher and later Canadian pro football teams who occasionally dropped into Michigan for state or national paddleball and racquetball tournaments. Bob, all-Canadian halfback at the 1971 national paddleball tournament in Flint, Michigan, good-naturedly slammed my head into the side wall with the heel of his hand during the coin toss, saying, 'Good luck, kiddo.' That inspired my first national singles title, where my partner and I also knocked the incumbent champion McNamara brothers, Bob and Bernie, off the court in doubles. It was ill-fated as the night before the finals the McNamaras had sent a 'Dewey defeats Truman' premature article and photo with borrowed trophies to the local newspaper, with the caption 'Bob and Bernie win National Doubles!'

In another opening at the 1974 Outdoor Nationals at Orange Coast College, a lob north of San Diego, I arrived late on a local bus to my match with three-time national wrestling champ Myron Roderick. Myron was already serving 3-0 on the outdoor court, and I asked for a warm up having never played the sport. Roderick lifted me over his head like a propeller on a beanie in a dizzying airplane spin, and served me onto the court to make the point,´ Get to the match on time!'

Chess players for centuries have been throwing pieces and hitting each other over the head in the openings to establish an edge, like the *fers* (queen) head. The lesson of chess in sport is that you may topple the king and start a new game.

Middle Game
3

After the open in chess or sport comes the middle game.

The prime difference between chess and sport on this matter is that the latter is aerobic and takes a toll after the open. The chess middle game comes somewhere around *move* twenty, and at about 10-10 in racquetball. The rain of sweat and mistakes threatens combinations making this stages of a sport the most likely for improvement.

Errors fall into two categories: Physical and mental, and the same may be said for life. Physical errors in rackets occur when you miss a shot due to a poorly practiced swing or footwork - anything not having to do with a mistake in shot selection. Mental errors, on the other hand, are the result of faulty brainwork. This is usually in shot selection, and an example is setting up to make a shot and at the last instant taking an inferior one. The cause of mental errors may be an untrained mind, a trained mind that hasn't practiced to empower the body, a psych out, lapse of focus, and most often my old friend fatigue.

Fatigue in the mid-games of football, soccer, car racing, martial arts, rackets, and especially individual sports begets mistakes. In the instant replays, the gallery churns over 'forced errors' where one player or team hems the other with strategy and shots to pry the error. What the bleachers often miss is that a sweep of forced errors was triggered long ago, perhaps in the opening, to tire the opposition into yielding these points.

The best forced tournament errors may begin the night before in romance when one player delivers to his next-day opponent a friendly knock on the door that opens to a pretty face, or to a mysterious complimentary fifth of Chivas Regal. This happened too frequently at early racquetball nationals, or, as in the case of national champs Bill Schmidtke to Charlie Brumfield, a box Godiva's chocolates.

You may tell a weary opponent in the warm-up or open up by his early fatigue, or in mid-game by your personal effort to run him, when he begins to stumble with the telltale first of inexplicable errors from favorable positions. This is the moment to bear down. If you are ever in his bind, the quick fixes are a timeout, long serve, fake injury timeout, or simply walk off the court betting that a timid ref will not forfeit you.

Bobby Fischer said, 'I like to make them squirm.' I liked to give them heart attacks. Once I came close in running a torrid gamesman so ragged he fell in the back court and appeared near death. Then, in the 1979 paddleball nationals, Marty Hogan turned the tables when I slumped in a rear corner unable to gasp, and he patted my shoulder and called 'timeout' for me.

Fischer played tennis regularly in defense of sport in chess. A 1972 photo at a La Costa, Ca. tournament shows him smashing a forehand serve in convincing form with an out-spin twist, great height, and flying hair.

This is the common ground of chess in sport for the middle game:

- The middle game is the core of chess and sport with all the combinational attacks and defenses brewing that sweep into the end game.

- Physical errors in strokes have nothing to do with luck; they are from lack of practice.

- Mental errors are not unfortunate but caused by time or score pressure, unfamiliarity with a position or shot, distractions, fatigue, nervous tension, overestimating an opponent, excessive caution or a cavalier style, maniac zest, or succumbing to gamesmanship.

- Books and articles on the openings and ends abound, but there is a dearth on the middle game since it is little understood and difficult.

- If a chess and sport statistician were to satisfy his curiosity over the weight of the open, middle and end games in determining the victor, he would conclude that the middle game is the decisive stage.

- The only thing more ruinous in the middle game than mistakes is routine.

- There are blunders all over board and a court waiting to be made.

- The number of unnecessary errors by all the players at chess move 20 and racquetball at score 10-10 in the second game is atrocious.

- Build your game around not making mistakes rather than fantastic shots.

- A player genuinely destroys himself who takes more pleasure from the number of points scored than the tally of physical and mental errors.

- After a mistake there is no need to become annoyed and think the game is lost; instead, recover balance with a shift in serve, shots, or pace.

- Chart your mistakes to correct them, and soon there is no more chart.

- The more mistakes there are in a game the lower the division of play.

- The primary task for closely matched players is to reach a playable middle game when the adrenalin has settled into the liver.

- If you play against yourself it will be more difficult to become overconfident.

- Every champion made all the mistakes you have.

*Bobby Fischer serves during a celebrity tennis game in
California in June 1972.*

My most flawless match was an ironic two-game loss
against the legend Marty Hogan on Denver Sorting House
glass, like a fishbowl, where the ball vaporized off the
strings and reappeared almost in my astonished mouth.
Again and again, in a sum 82 points, I counted zero mental
and one physical error. The scores were 21-20, 21-20.

An even better match defines the Physical vs. Mental
Errors Hypothesis, a few years earlier. I had observed my
early round Chicago dark horse for five minutes, liked his
grace and verve during the warm up, and on walking onto
the court for our match I wished to beat as well as coach
him. 'I'll tell you what,' I offered flatly with the
handshake, 'And you need not listen. I will hit every shot in
the first game as follows: Every deep court forehand is a

cross-court pass, every front court forehand is a kill to the right front corner, every backhand is the same in reverse for the respective positions, and for all killshots if I am closer to either side wall it will be down-the-line, or from closer the centerline then a pinch. Every shot taken above shoulder height will go to the ceiling. Now you have the game book on me, knowing where every shot will go, and it will do no good. Except for a demonstration of the efficacy of shot selection.' He wisely declined a $100 bet, and took a 20-10 lesson of a lifetime.

An illusive aspect of mistakes is the sacrifice. The chess sacrifice is common, to give a pawn for a position, or for a knight, five moves in the future that the opponent doesn't see. In racquetball, sacrifices are fewer since one in a 21-point game may turn a match. The first rule of racket sacrifice is to make it on your serve in order to lose not the point but the side out. Many hustlers win against an unaware thinking he must score only two points in a handicap game starting at 19-20, but the odds of him winning two subsequent rallies for a point are small. The instant a mistake or an inaccuracy occurs, the first thought against a strong player should be, 'Why am I being duped?

I sometimes use the ostensible mistakes of a lifted kill for a pass to test a rival's feet and breath, or to his deep court backhand to test the stroke. In clinics i opened the service lesson with a Z-serve that reflected into my third-eye to get attention.

Combinations

4

A chess combination is a sequence of moves, often initiated by a sacrifice, opponent's blunder, or curveball. The combinations, like of a lock, leave the other fellow few options each step of the way and results in a tangible gain of points or position. More deeply, at most points in chess or sport each player has several options from which to choose to make the next move or series of moves. One first learns the single moves, then the combinations... until entering a game against a master means knowing waves of moves within tides of play, that all fall under the name combinations.

The purpose of combinations is not only immediate points and position, but in bringing more pressure on the opposition to try to think hard and lose track of his own bank of combinations. Paul Morphy, the 'Pride and Sorrow of Chess', like most sport prodigies played quickly and was hard to beat. His 1858 'Opera Game' is considered one of the most beautiful attacking games ever to demonstrate how to use time, develop pieces and generate threats. He was the unofficial World Chess Champion of the 19th century having vanquished all serious competition, and declared he would play no more matches without giving odds of a pawn and move. Hats and cigars were named after him, and he was the first sports figure to issue a commercial endorsement when he declared of a watch, 'I have examined the contents of this watch and find it to be made of 100% machinery.' Machinery is aggressive, the wearer became the web, and finding no worthy opponents Morphy was eventually persecuted by imaginary relatives. He went into seclusion with a reputation of a fetish for women's shoes and paced the porch at night repeating, 'The city is conquered and the little king will go away looking sheepish'. At age 47 in New Orleans, on taking a cold bath with the door locked, a doctor later opened it and pronounced him dead from 'congestion of the brain'.

Since combinations is a high variations game after a simple prologue and before a targeted end, it falls squarely into the mid-game. The true colors of fitness begin to wear in the middle game that factor into combinations for the first time since the open. My technique was to ride out a high energy 'bull' in the open till his energy waned and then try to pick him to pieces with combinations. As a novice climbs to advanced levels, he too discovers that physical fitness equalizes, mental errors diminish, and combinations win or lose the match.

Combinations are the essence of *any* advanced sport where the brain injects a sequence of events rather than knee-jerk response toward winning a point, game or, if thinking far ahead, a match. In fencing this is clearly illustrated by a Tactical Wheel of thrusts and parries. In wrestling combinations are called chains where one first tries a double leg takedown that, if thwarted, develops into a fireman's carry and always looking for an ankle trip. In boxing it's the old left jab, right cross, and left uppercut. In tennis a power serve to the backhand tape precedes a rush to overhead slam at the net to a vacant forehand.

At the highest levels of 'intent', combinations within combinations interlace beautifully and mathematically. The most combinational players I've faced in all sports are market traders, pilots, computer programmers, mathematicians, and attorneys whose daily use of combinations make them formidable.

Here are the common denominators of combination in chess and sport:

- After a century discussion in Soviet literature on the correct definition, it was decided a combination is a forced variation with a sacrifice; as in rackets where one foregoes putting the ball away in favor of analyzing and exhausting the opponent.

- Fatigue is the pin of sports.

- Combinations are delayed gratification.

- Once there is the slightest hint of combinational possibilities on the board or court, look for unusual moves to solve them.

- Winning combinations are born from good positions, and by a good position I am in the right place at the right time.

- The characteristic mark of a chess combination is

surprise for the defender, not for the assailant.

- Combinations in anything encourage creative play to solve the maze of variations.

- Combinations are more difficult to work out in defending than attacking.

- Some combinations come intuitively and others after labor; but most of their counters come after the match.

Fatigue stirred into combinations is deadly to the thought process unless one steps out for fresh air. This was illustrated when Harlem Globetrotter Ron Rubenstein and golden gloves boxer Charley Drake teamed for racquetball doubles. The opposition repeatedly angled ceiling balls to the weaker player, Drake, until in the tiebreaker game Rubenstein walked out the court door, got a drink of water, and reentered a minute later during same rally.

A strong combinational player is a poker-faced bitch in the starting blocks, and tries forceful moves in his mind that will trigger weak responses. The first move of a strong sequence evokes an unexpected re-assessment that may be read in the foe's body reposition to reassess that he may live through the next point. Unless you see several moves ahead on the boards of life - cards, business negotiations, social interactions, back alleys, nature survivals, and most sports - you are doomed to the smaller ranks. But if you practice long enough at any task to learn the common variations, and add a few of your own to suit personality, then the life arena becomes a canvas to paint color schemes knowing, more or less, what the final picture will look like.

Combinations have always been the most intriguing aspect of chess in sport. The masters search for them, the public applauds them, the critics appraise, and it's an enjoyable circus because combinations carried to the highest transcend even mathematics, computers, and approach poetry and music. The great pleasure is that a human mind is behind them.

It takes practice.

Practice

5

As the pianist practices the most complicated pieces to improve his finger techniques, I practiced the most difficult shots in racquetball. One was the drive serve with a hatful of balls or an agreeable mate who wished to practice the returns; and the other that was the focus for one full year was the volley. Learn the volley and every other part of the game falls into place.

Practice includes conditioning. My regimen while living in racquetball Mecca San Diego for six years during the Golden Era 70s was to daily:

- Ride a bicycle twenty miles into an offshore breeze.
- Run 7 miles from Crystal Pier to the Ocean Beach jetty on the Pacific beach.
- Hike up to Gorham's sports Center for two hours of games, one hour of solitaire practice, and thirty minutes of weights.
- And then ride back home into an off-land breeze.

No one except a little fellow called Mini-Hippy could outlast me on the court, and if I kept honing the shots via practice I erroneously considered myself unbeatable.

The solo one hour practice time was halved from

apprentice years where I learned that when you practice the things you know you learn things you don't know. A corollary is practicing things you don't know to explore new strokes, techniques and strategy.

On busting a leg one year, I left crutches for a month outside the court door and learned to hit standing upright with a walking cast, and saw a strategic advantage as opposers watched me set upright for a shot like the Tin Woodsman, and rocked backward on their heels as blazing killshots burned holes in the bottom board.

The best practice game for stamina is 'squash racquetball' where a tape or chalk line is drawn across the front wall about two-feet above the floor and all serves and shots must hit above the line or the service/point is lost. Rallies of sixty-or-more shots are not uncommon and a game to five points may last up to two hours. You are promised many happy returns on forgotten or unexplored spin and pass secrets.

The analogue of Baring Chess is where there is no checkmate and the game is won by the player who captures all of his opponent's pieces, leaving him with only a bare king. This game was played as early as the 9th century, and many think the Baring Game was the original of chess.

Round robins are another strong trainer where eight players occupying four courts play single games to fifteen and rotate until everyone has played each other. In the drunken version, at some point, a break is taken to determine who has scored the least points and does not get to drink.

Simultaneous exhibitions in chess and sports have a long history even before I took out the MSU football offensive and defensive coaches one-on-two in a paddleball exhibition. They crashed in center court covering pinches trickling just out of reach, and lost a little money. Later, I added more simultaneous games on the court including many San Diego Chargers football players, and discovered that the more the merrier for the sole practitioner unless the team gets wise and places two large outposts in each front corner to block and cover killshots.

A truer form of simultaneous exhibition in rackets or any individual sport is one player taking on a string of comers one-by-one in short 11-point games with no rests between. This is excellent instruction for a clinic of up to twenty players who rotate into the 'play-the-pro' court alongside their own games on outer courts. And, after each game that may last ten minutes, as in chess exhibitions, the student gets a two-minute critique as the teacher catches his breath. The tip to all is to play aggressively, for 95% of all victims in simultaneous displays owe their defeat to their own passivity. The simultaneous-giver lacks the time to work out the variations of hawkish play. On psychological grounds, too, aggressively approaching the simul-giver or any strong opponent is a sound strategy and at the root of nearly every historic upset in all sports.

Joseph Henry Blackburne, with a large black beard, strong temper and whisky at the chessboard, enjoyed success giving blindfold and simultaneous exhibitions of wide open and technical play that earned him the respectful title 'Black Death'. During one exhibition at Cambridge University, the students thought to gain the advantage by placing a bottle of whisky at each end of the playing ovals; however, in the end he emptied both bottles and won all the games in record time. Blackburne's fondness for drinking whisky at the board once led him to down an opponent's glass, and shortly afterward the opponent resigned, leading him to quip, 'My opponent left a glass of whisky en prise and I took it en passant.' The general public flocked to watch an estimated 100,000 career games of lightning play with fits of temper including a loss to Wilhelm Steinitz, the first undisputed world champion, after which instead of tipping the king Blackburne threw the five-foot Steinitz out the window.

You see chess matches throughout Humphrey Bogart films because, before becoming a movie star, he hustled strangers at 5-minute chess for 50-cents a game in New York Times Square chess parlors, parks and Coney Island. He played cast and crew between Hollywood sets and in real life in tournaments one level below master. The famous *Casablanca* chess scene hadn't been in the original script but was put there at his insistence from a position of one of his correspondence games. The FBI in 1943 prevented him from playing postal chess thinking the chess notation was secret codes, as Blackburne had been arrested as a spy for sending chess moves in the mail. Bogart drew one game in a simultaneous exhibition with American chess grandmaster Samuel Rehevsky, and appeared on a 1945 cover of Chess Review that I saw years later as a kid after I gave up rounds of funny books.

My first chess book was on Al Horowitz's openings, and the second was a collection of challenging positions. I was attracted to positional play in taking a move or shot from a certain position, always the same from that spot, even if the opponent anticipated it. No argument against this ever beat me. Positional play was hammered into my childhood reality by a comic book of super-heroes donning basketball uniforms to play against a villainous visiting team, and an elf dropped in from the 5th-dimension to coach the heroes to mark X's on the court and always go to those spots to shoot unerring winners. The good guys always won in the funnies.

The one racquetball player I didn't like and admired the most was Steve Strandemo whom I caught after hours before our next day's Oceanside pro match in a tournament court marking the floors and walls with sundry little x's for where to hit from and aim to. The marks were indelible and he didn't win that one because I used the spots too.

There is solitary practice in both chess and sport. And there are practice games against opponents. The proper ratio is about 1:1 during the amateur years, and 1:2 in the advanced, and always against an equal or stronger player. I preferred entering the court tired from a bicycle or jog in order to suffer the combinations under tournament energy. Chess masters have a reputation for blending the physical with mental, with daily bicycling, shadow boxing, followed by a cold plunge, and then walk briskly into the chess club to play their seconds and coaches.

Coach

A bizarre stage arose outside a Miami racquetball court during a timeout when a person approached who was my mirror - dual colored Converse Chucks, a mop of blonde curls, and he greeted with a wry smile, 'My name is Bo Two!' I nodded dumbly. I prefer him now as Bo One, my life coach.

Bo Champagne moved to six states (Louisiana, Missouri, Kansas, Texas, Colorado and South Dakota) to win state championships in each in one or more divisions. He carried his LSU chess set with him between matches for pick-up games, and as a training tool for kids' clinics. Now Bo follows the pro circuits like the good Lincoln penny you see in every gallery, looking about like me, quietly observing the matches, and kibitzing. At each event, he identifies the most promising youngster and takes him into a court with racquet and chess set for a thirty minute lesson. Afterward, the racquetball sprite packs his gym bag and thumbs or buses to the next tournament... Then one morning Bo Champagne played blitz bicycle against a 40mph truck and was nearly totaled. Yet he phoenixed as a traveling grandmaster and an inspiration for this book.

To matriculate into a chess-in-sport grandmaster whose understanding is superior to the thousands of ordinary players and even some pros, you develop many tricks cloaked in artistry with a cool, calm mind. The professional who has best exhibited this to me is the great racquetballer Cliff Swain who glides around the court like a Praying Mantis suddenly springing to set to stroke and kill and kill again.

Swain's game was sculpted in the South Boston L Street 60'-long outdoor courts known as the Graveyard of Champions. There vied also Mr. Universe Mike 'The Mighty' Quinn, and handball's best Paul Haber and Jim Jacobs, along with many roving racquetball champs who lost to tough local Bostonians there. Marty Hogan is the only 'outsider' to ever have come in and win a tournament at the L. 60'-long courts with a ceiling going back twenty feet from the front wall.

Swain steps out as a cross between an ascetic monk and predator from a long list of national champions who I played and beat – except Cliff - and occasionally losing to all of the pioneers from the game's inception in the late 60's through its maturity in the mid-80s. Yet I couldn't have touched Swain on my best day. The only slight against Swain is the early greats approached perfection without coaches because there were none.

Champs or not, sooner or later the body salts pools on the hardwood, and tactics long ago abandoned in lactic acid, the cherished strategies you practiced a thousand times earlier do not come to mind. This is the Fatigue Factor. Now, it helps to have a coach in the gallery, or a crib sheet of backup plays on the side of your gym bag to peek at through the back glass. Hollywood stunt star (for Captain Kirk, etc.) and top-16 pro Jay Jones wore what many thought was a hearing aid for many years, until one day in the locker room he spoke into a urinal, 'What Donna?' and it was an earpiece to receive instruction from his professional girlfriend.

Unless a player *groks* chess with a rating of at least 2400, the significant knowledge he can impart to others is limited, and the same is true in sport. Choose a coach who's older and tournament seasoned. Many of the pioneer racket pros now stand backstage among the modern title holders, having taught what they wanted - not so much to teach as how to learn. There is nothing like being floored on learning the depth of a codger master, by identifying the elderly man with a gimp and callused hand nodding approvingly again and again as if recalling through Alzheimer's his own peak moments.

The strange story of Abjeeb the Chess Automation begins in 1865 with a Bristol cabinet maker who built a life-size figure in yellow turban and flowing red rob in which 1894 US Chess Champion Albert Hodges got his first job as a hidden operator. He played checkers for a dime, and a game of chess for 25-cents, in 900+ games that lost only three times, and never lost a checker game. A sore loser shot Abjeeb in the torso and supposedly wounded an operator before Hodges, but several knew the apprentice had been killed. To cover up for the still successful automation, they had disposed of the apprentice's body and, due to the transient hobo nature of the apprentice with no reputable sources, the murder was never solved and Abjeeb continued his win streak.

I was fascinated by Ajeeb and for a 9th grade science fair constructed 'Mr. Marvel', a shoebox filled with erector set parts and sewing spindles that spew out a little mouth between cardboard ears the best catseye marbles from my collection to answer math puzzles. The automation won a red ribbon that significantly led to a next term appointment in a 1964 vanguard FORTRAN class where we trooped after school three times a week to write programs, punch them onto cards, and feed into a large whirring box that reeked of ozone but produced accurate answers that I never dreamed possible.

If a machine can be made to imitate humans, then the reverse seems true that a human can dare to become a machine in sports. And that's how I became a cold, calculating player. I was warm off the court, but found that the most winning way in sports was to pattern after Ajeeb. By the turn of the century, another operator complained of odd occurrences inside Ajeeb where the automation was moving of its own accord. Shortly after, it was allegedly destroyed in a fire on Coney Island.

I didn't picture myself as a grandmaster, to say nothing of aspiring to little chess and early racquetball trophies that I had whittled, and glued on gold-plates from Goodwill Industries. A grandmaster or national champion, in my little mind, existed in a different world and weren't even people but gods and heroes. However, as Abraham Lincoln advised, 'I will prepare and someday my chance shall come.' I became an instructor.

I was perhaps the first in the country in 1972 to charge for lessons, courtesy of one evening's tutorial on how to teach strokes, serves and strategies in Dr. Bud Muehleison's San Diego living room. He concluded with the brash suggestion to walk cold into George Brown's 70th Street Racquet Club and ask to become their first club pro. 'What's a club pro?' I asked, but nonetheless called on Browns the next day and got the job. I was a hayseed veterinarian, whose California misplaced State Board exam forced me into a racquetball teaching job, splitting the take with the club, and a year later the first professional tour launched and I had found a new career.

Overnight racquetball became *the* sport of the 1970's, where I profited with the nation's first clinics and camp. These were the first professional coaching where the attendees included cross-over pro athletes, Hollywood stars, mafia, government agents, beauty queens, and stoned college students. When clinic sponsors were strapped for cash, as in 19th century England chess exhibitions that paid with cases of Scotch, I collected a hundred pounds of granola, 500-pounds of Purina Dog Chow, a tour of the Lansing Box and New Jersey Garden Way factories, books, designer clothes, and a car. I opened Latin America to racquetball with the first international clinic tour with Chelsea George by bus and train. In 1976, DBI published *The Complete Book of Racquetball* to a hungry market that bought 200,000, with instruction coming full circle as coaches read it to answer new credentialing questions after noting the book's dedication, 'To Carl Loveday who begat Muehleisen who begat Brumfield.'

Chess preceded sport everywhere. Russian grandmaster Efim Bogolubow played for the world championship twice in a career spanning forty-four years and the Bogolubow-Indian defense was named after him. At the beginning of WW I, he was taken prisoner while playing in a German tournament along with other strong Russian players like Alekhine. They subsequently played eight world-class 'Tournaments of Prisoners', and Bogolubow wrote a series of books to which he annotated, 'The young people have read my book. Now I have no chance.' Learning from that mistake, after writing *The Complete Book of Racquetball*, I had a surprisingly good time revealing counters to the pros who had read it.

Coaching parallels of chess and sport are:

- An ounce of common sense from the sidelines may outweigh a pound of variations on the board or court.

- Coaches should be used as glasses to assist the sight but not replace it.

- Chess players have 'seconds' and racket players coaches - all have kibitzers who are selectively valuable.

- Every great master finds it useful to have a few personal theories which he keeps to himself.

- The masters think themselves immune from the surprises of theory.

Throughout racquetball, I was playing speed chess with Charles Drake and Ray Bayer, the president and factory foreman of the lead manufacturer Leach Industries, on our La Jolla, California patio with Neil Diamond singing, 'Have you ever heard about the frog who dreamed of being a king, and then became one?'

Sometimes on an acrophobic pedestal, I am asked, 'Coach, improve my game by five points in five minutes?' I reply easily with tactics and strategies.

Tactics

7

Tactics is a system of details of response to X situation, whereas strategy is a more general term for planning to sport or war. The salesperson's tactics greet each customer, but his strategic maxim is to seem always to agree with the customer. Tactics are the employable nuances of strategy and, to me, more valuable.

Successful players at sport, travel, business, and even crime and criminal solving develop a tactical instinct for what is possible or likely, and what is not worth calculating. However, the winners of life are like the major league pitcher with an archive of resultant pitches for each batter, or the good doctor with a catalogue of remedies for every condition. General strategies kick in when an exacting tactic cannot be found.

The tactician must know what to do whenever something needs doing, whereas the strategist projects what to do when nothing needs doing. The former is a computer programmer on the hoof, and the latter is creative. My goal is to have a tactic for every situation in life, while others prefer the exhilaration of ad-libs. Willie Sutton had both as the most famous bank robber in history, until mated by the FBI on arrest in 1952 with a copy in his possession of *How to Think Ahead in Chess* by Horowitx.

Tactics start with what's available, analyze for flaws, and if there are none then study the ones all others smile at, however absurd they look at first glance. In this manner, I developed the stroke technique of always hitting in an awkward position rather than with a model stroke that may be read like large font. Also, I deceived by looking exactly the opposite direction from the target.

Sport tactics are a headache to compose by greenhorns in their first few months, but afterward the dividends last a lifetime. Chess is 99% tactics, but racquetball is about 25%, with the other quarters going to strokes, strategies and fitness.

Tactical similarities of chess and sport include:

- The defensive power of a pinned piece is imaginary, and so is the zeal of an unfit athlete.

- 'Tactics flow from a superior position', said Bobby Fischer and Charlie Brumfield.

- Play the move that forces the won point in the simplest way.

- After you counter a move or shot a fleeting series of variations passes in the mind and the best eye selects and performs the next.

- Half the variations which are calculated in a tournament match turn out to be completely superfluous, but no one knows in advance which half.

- To free your game, take off some of your adversary's men. In rackets pass up opportunities to end rallies to run him so he may no longer complicate the game with thoughtful combinations.

- Chess masters have said to play the position itself, not some abstract idea of the position. In court sports play the reality of the position and don't get lost in the abstract that seems more fetching.

- Never rely on a bluff.

- When your King is under attack don't worry about losing a pawn on the queenside, and when you are overly fatigued in a match give up your attack in front to rest with ceiling shots.

- Tactics requires execution; strategy requires thought.

My legacy to racquetball is not the Around-world or Z-balls that Charlie Brumfield and I pioneered in 1970 at MSU, nor the ceiling game borrowed from handball that my nemesis perfected to a T to wax me and the field for the next five years, but my contribution for all the sport gave me is the volley shot. A volley is hit out of the air on the serve return or rally before a floor bounce for three pluses: Surprise, a shorter shot, and the opponent is screened visually and physically from play. It's the most difficult shot in racquetball, however I practiced it fairly exclusively for one year and then took it to many finals matches. In one breath, the volleyer vs. himself sans-volley has an eight points spread in a game to 21. I remember the afternoon I introduced it in a practice match to top-16 pro Rich Wagner who shook his head on retiring from the court, 'I don't know what got into me today.' I used it to beat eventual world champ Mike Yellen, Jerry Hilecher, Steve Serot and the rest of the field for three months before someone like Wagner wised up and started using it, and thereafter the volley spell was broken. The average lag time before a new shot or strategy is infected by everyone on tour is three months, while they not only use it but develop a counter. Hence, tactics undergo continual evolution, but slowly, only if one keeps mum.

The 'Argentine Massacre' of 1955 illustrates the power of a new tactic rendered ineffectual in strong analysis. At an Interzonal chess tournament in Gothenburg, Sweden three Argentinean players developed a series of moves to use against the ascendant Russian players in the tournament. Astonishingly, the three Argentineans found themselves playing against Russians in round 14 where their maneuver worked, and all three Russians seemed struck at the same time. A half-hour later, one of the Russians figured out a three-move counter that the Argentineans hadn't anticipated, and as soon as he played it the others watching on followed suit, and soon the Russians had knocked down all three Argentineans like dominos.

Chess, sport and life are inconceivable without tactics.

Strategy
8

Progressing from tactics to strategy, the former is specific replies and the latter is a plan, plus backup plan, to win.

A simple strategy that presents the most complications to the opponent so as the game winds up to the final point, with the competitors drenched in sweat and defaulting to deep habits, is my idea of the top strategy.

In about 1973, I encountered an interesting gray area in strategy that demanded simplification for success. One simply cannot in sport execute a difficult strategy in the throes of fatigue and psychological duress. A method was required that worked in the worst case scenario, every time. I conceived the Offensive Theory of Play. It, as much as anything I did, instantly won multiple paddleball and racquetball titles.

The Theory forces action by always taking the most offensive shot: Kill, if not possible then Pass, if not possible then Ceiling. Then I lost solely to gamesmen who could orchestrate the gallery and ref into stalling, a la the wait-to-death on a challenger who refuses the chess clock. The Offensive Theory is an initial strategy for the novice to becoming an open player that develops exact repeating shots from specific spots on the court.

Wilhelm Steinitz became the world number one in an all-out attacking style that was common in late 1800's chess. He won the first official world championship match in 1886, and it would be another 13 years before anyone could defeat him; not even Blackburne who threw him out the window for beating and spitting on him. The first world championship was held in the USA with the first five games played in New York, the next four in St. Louis, and the final eleven in New Orleans. His daughter sold programs and photographs to spectators during the New York phase to earn a few extra dollars for the family, unable to afford a winter coat as she stood shivering in the vestibule in the cold January weather. Steinitz held the world championship for 27 years until, after he lost the title, he showed signs of mental illness in challenging God to a match and occasionally beat him at chess with pawn odds. He died in the East River mental asylum on New York's Ward Island, penniless.

And everyone has his pet play when the chips are down. With Charlie Brumfield it was a crack ace serve to the forehand. Vic Niederhoffer hit the courageous 3-wall boast to gain match point against Hogan at the 1975 Las Vegas stop. My 'discovered check' may now be revealed as the backhand overhead reverse pinch kill from deep left court along the longest 45-foot hypotenuse of the court to dead roll in the right front.

The strategic collective of chess and sport are:

- The best stamp of strategy is simplicity.

- The truest strategy is always change a losing game and never change a winning game.

- In chess, sport and life play an alert aggressive approach and never without a backup strategy.

- In the open play like a book, in the mid-game play like a magician, and in the ending play like a machine.

- Play for complications in a game only when you have an overall plan.

- It's better to follow a plan consistently even if it isn't the best one than to slug aimlessly.

- When you think you have a good strategy, look for a better one.

- When you find a plan, look for a counter-plan.

- When you find a plan with no counter, make a backup plan.

- If you like to attack, remove the obstacles the gamesman puts in your way by ignoring them.

- Never make a move, hit a serve or shot that you don't know how to refute, thus ensuring the whole game.

- When everything on the board is so clear that your

opponent cannot see it, conceal your thoughts from everyone.

- The center of the board is the center of the court where the first principle of attack! dominates.

- As long as the rival has not yet castled on each move seek a pretext for an offensive; and if the opponent doesn't challenge for center court force play with kills.

- Play on both sides of the board and service line distinguishes the amateur and pro.

- A win by an unsound strategy, such as mental errors at the profit of powerful strokes, is criminal and ends in future loses.

- The number of points that can be gained by correct move and shot selections are underestimated.

- When you play against a wall - a player who exploits all the defensive resources at his command - you must walk along a narrow path of 'the only move'.

- A plan is made for the whole game, and a plan for a few moves.

- Never install a strategy into a key match until it's practiced a thousand times.

- When things get too complicated go to the pure attack or the pure defense.

Daring ideas are best in chess in sport as the men move forward, that may be beaten but they may also start a winning game.

Vienna grandmaster and chess writer Rudolph Spielmann was a lawyer, like Charlie Brumfield, who never worked as one except while playing sport. Spielmann was known as 'The Last Knight of the King's Gambit', my favorite opening, and 'The Master of Attack', my favorite theory. His daredevil play was full of sacrifices and brilliances that astonished the greater players of the early 20th century. Had he only refereed my Chicago pro finals against Brumfield and intoned his famous, 'A good sacrifice is one that is not necessarily sound but leaves your opponent dazed and confused,' i would have won and stuck to the spiritual side of racquetball. Instead I retired from the game to a Michigan garage.

A common sacrifice in old school racquetball was passing up killshots to extend rally after rally with beyond-touch passes to tire the rival until, as Brumfield, he fell into a cramped heap in back court. Spielmann would have forfeited Brumfield as he rolled out the door into the hall and disappeared into the concrete YMCA bowels. Instead, after an hour, he recoiled craftily to tie me into leg and arm knots from trying to find him for an hour.

It was part of the ploy. In a match, forced play winds and winds you through a labyrinth of variations where tactics break down due to sheer numbers and fatigue, and general strategies must kick in until the situation becomes familiar again. Charlie Brumfield's cheat sheet lay under his grip of his old wooden Marcraft handle that had seen so many finals, but only once each year would he resort to tearing the grip off, call 'Equipment time-out', and staring at the bare handle scream, 'Loveday Autograph Model', and read whatever other instructions for the match were written under the signature of the godfather of Racquetball, his coach Carl Loveday.

If you could only see inside a grandmaster's mind there would be a course of thought and action called a *plan* which is the sum total of successive strategic operations which are each carried out according to separate ideas arising from the demands of the position. Likewise, in racquetball, the plan is shot selection according to the place of stroke on the court, and less so the score, fatigue, and opponent's position, that form a string of winning shots.

Shot selection is as simple as the nose on your face. There are 400 different possible chess positions after one move each, and likewise in rackets one may calculate the reasonable shot selections following the service and return. In racquetball it is only eight. 'Deep Thought' was once the strongest chess playing computer in the world in searching two million chess positions per second and became the first computer to defeat a grandmaster in tournament play by beating Bent Larsen at the 1988 US Open, and the next year became the world computer champion. There are 72,084 different possible positions after two moves each on the chessboard, and over 288 billion different possibilities after four moves each. The number of distinct 40-moves in a game is far greater than the number of electrons in the observable universe. Meanwhile, in racquetball there are only eight repeated strong shot selections throughout each rally that are dependant on the six quadrants of the court: On the right side the front, middle and back court; and the same on the left side. From each of these quadrants, by following positional play and the Offensive Theory of Play, every time one sets to swing, really very little goes through the mind except to execute one of eight shots: Kill, Pass or Ceiling to either side, plus an infrequent Z or around-world ball. The total possibilities in racquetball are 48, and not Deep Thought at all to win at chess in sport.

Shot selection was so easy in early racquetball that I had to cloak it to prevent imitation with the Look-The-Other-Way stroke. In chess, this is called the Idea of Key-Move at just the reverse of what a player in 999 out of 1000 could look for. On every stroke I stepped and looked the opposite way to which the ball was headed; for example, a down-line kill was costumed to be a cross-court pass that split the rival like a wishbone.

Key strategic points should be protected by under-use and by laying back until a pivotal point in a match. My seldom-seen trick was a backhand wallpaper serve clinging a couple of inches along the left side wall from front to back that could neither be taken on the fly nor off the back wall. It had to be returned after a fussy bounce from shoulder high that broke many racquet frames, and led to arguments of did the equipment break before or after the ace? This single shot more than any other won tournament finals. The problem was that once a ruse like it defeats a specific player he took it home to find a counter, and practiced a thousand times until it was no longer A-Keeley's heel.

After one such win I wrote a sham article for *International Racquetball* magazine called the 'Mickey Mouse Theory' professing to hit this wallpaper serve utilizing a mantra to relax the mind to enable the steady hand. After publication, I sat on the left side glass tournament walls and watched players silently mouth 'Mickey Mouse' to imitate the serve, but actually the secret was in the spin.

The greatest trick shot I ever saw was a Chicago gymnast turned semi-pro player who did cartwheels and flips around the court and kicked me in the chin to block my coverage.

Strategy building is magic in pulling rabbits out the hat to amaze the audience. This was the secret of the first international champs who necessarily were the best strategists the game will ever know - world badminton champ Loveday who coached Muehleisen to 69 titles who instructed Brumfield to supersede them. A tip of the hat to roly-poly Loveday, Mule with zero backhand, and Brumfield sans service that their steak-and beer all night hashes in the lobby of America's first private Pacific Paddleball Association court pulled out strategic rabbits that escaped and multiplied onto today's courts.

How would the old champs have fared against the new? Given a leveling of equipment - balls and racquets - if you just brought them back from the dead they wouldn't do well. However, on adjusting for three months they will have strategized and practiced to hold their own. The same is in reverse for a modern champ flung into the PPA and old YMCA dungeons where eye guards battled spider webs, mouth guards vs. follow-throughs, and a rain of balls fell from light fixtures after a ceiling strike.

My old MSU wrestling coach Grady Penninger used to berate us, 'Practice a move a thousand times on the mat before you use it in a tournament. Once you have the strokes and serves, and know some combinations, tactics and strategies, and have practiced each a thousand times, it's time to start thinking about entering a tournament.

Tournament

------------------------------------*9*------------------------------------

The worlds of chess and sport are obligated to organize matches between players at all levels to introduce new blood, promote, make a pecking order, determine the best in a region or the world as inspirations, and as business per usual. I know this from having organized two small chess tournaments, a handful of paddleball and racquetball events, and having grown up from day one with professional racquetball.

The first pro stop was in 1974, with a half-dozen more that year in the inaugural pro tour with a $1500 purse for 1st-3rd places. This meager amount, comparable to what Art Bisguier earned in the 1950s for simultaneous exhibition tours, was a godsend to anyone accustomed to practicing and playing for tournament T-shirts. I hitched, bicycled, bussed or hoboed freights to each to accumulate a down payment on a '74 Chevy van, dubbed the Blue Lemon, that was fashioned into a a tournament van with cushions on wall-to-wall carpeting and four speakers, ice box, chessboards, and a library. The Blue Lemon carted players to tournaments around the West for years often with my second, Fillmore Hare, a 7-foot stuffed rabbit, riding shotgun with an invisible fishline attached to his hand to wave down fascinating people.

The early pros in the van talked about adapting a ranking system like the chess FIDE to ensure there will always be a just world champion. It wasn't, and the 1970's and 80s tournaments were fixed by habitual tinkers in seeding, referees, balls, and choice of courts. A key element in the graft was the tournament director who selected a batch of fast balls to put in a sauna to heat up before explosive matches, and pioneer pros who favored a slower chess-like game countered his ploy with ice cube baths or by slitting their game balls with razors, or drawing a few cc's of air with hypodermic needles. Not every tournament was arranged, but it was the rule of the day to ensure that the sponsors and association's darlings won. I was no darling wearing a 'Spay that Bitch' tournament shirt (to promote veterinary medicine), and was the quasi-attorney for hire to dissect tournament rules to level the playing field.

A 1962 Bobby Fischer article in *Sports Illustrated* 'The Russians Have Fixed World Chess' foreshadowed racquetball world tournament play. Russian control of chess had reached a point where there could be no honest competition for the world championship. The system set up by the governing body of world chess ensured that there will always be a Russian world champion because only a Russian can win the preliminary tournament that determines his challenger. Likewise, the racquetball qualifying satellite events of the 1980's prevented any player outside the sponsor-association loop to enter the world championship.

Myriad spitting battles emerged from the politics, but the

best kept secret recently told me by a high IRA (International Racquetball Association) official is the backroom deal between the IRA and manufacturer Ektelon that switched racquetball into what you see on TV today. The #1 Leach manufacturer of racquets with its stable of pros was taking the lion's share from Ektelon. The IRA racquet dimension rules disallowed a big-head racquet, but suddenly in 1984 the first oversized Ektelon Contra series appeared and consistently won tournaments. While the length of the racquet remained the same, required 22-inches, the width of the face increased by several inches for a five-point edge per game that carved new secondary tournament champions. The masses grabbed the Ektelon big-heads, while across the country only the Leach pros were bound by their contracts to use the antiquated models. The IRA had quietly changed the dimension rule to coincide with Ektelon's completion of a costly tool-and-die for the first big head series. Ektelon flooded the market in the six months it took Leach to tool their own version of the oversize, but by that time Ektelon was the marketplace king and hundreds of new young pros streamed to the tournaments with the big heads to win. On a personal level, an ongoing duel between the Leach and Ektelon darlings, Marty Hogan and Mike Yellen, tipped to Yellen who had never previously won. 'Hogan is a screamer, and Yellen, a gentleman,' exacted the IRA official, and so the covert deal forever altered racquetball and its champions.

The racquetball association and sponsors for fifteen years played both black and white pieces that were the pros in what chess calls Helpmate, a problem in which both White and Black cooperate to find the shortest mate.

When world class racquetball players in the 1980's started being omitted from the championships, with many vowing never to compete again, but I was allowed to play as a formidable publicist for the sport. However, in protest, I began entering tournaments righty in pros and lefty in Opens. Once I nearly met myself in the finals of a Michigan tournament using an alias left-handed to come up the other side of the draw before losing in the semi's. Then I started playing the first game of pro matches left-handed, usually losing, and winning in the second and tiebreakers to take the match. It was like giving rook odds. At the Flint, Mi. stop the club owner, and later reigning IRA director, Jim Hiser protested with tongue in cheek that I 'quit clowning around' for the finals. Enter a clown with candy cane kneesocks and suspender balloon shorts striding past the convulsing bleachers onto the court. The face makeup dripping into my eyes nearly lost the sweaty tiebreaker.

Except for the fixes and starched jocks in the young brutish sport, I loved every other aspect that fell into the New Age nexus. There was spirituality, personal awakenings, and hash brownies in the competition club cooler. I was persuaded by aides to augment my game with acupuncture, meditation, mantras, and one endless loop tape that repeated each night for a month as I drifted through REM, 'Every day in every way you're getting better and better'.

I discarded these but could do nothing about the spiritual uplifting of mini-skirts of the natural times in the gallery behind the glass every time a rival got close for a shot. I paid these wall gals, and the Soviet chess parallel was the use of parapsychologists and yoga meditation experts in the audience to affect the minds of players, and the objections took years to resolve.

Daily, at San Diego's Mel Gorham's Sports Center, a hotshot east coaster with a sore thumb from hitchhiking blew up to the curb with his home in a gym bag, and a very competitive grin. He was pursuing the California Sports Dream. Their glad handshake prizes were replaced in short order by the hard currency of a few hundred bucks per pounding tournament after tournament. Most of these aspirants made more from their $30 sponsor per diems than from prize earnings. During my peak five-year mid-70s reign, I garnered an annual $5K in prize money, and equal in per diem, while cashing in plane tickets in favor of the Blue Lemon, there was $3k in shoe endorsements, $1K in book royalties, $10k in camps and clinics, and $1k in better's wagers for an annual sum of $25,000.

I was lucky, the first sponsored player by the first post-wood frame racquet manufacturer Trenway; the second sponsored player (after Bud Muehleisen) by the first steel racquet manufacturer Ektelon; and the first sponsored by the initial fiberglass composite manufacturer Leach. Then I lugged a 4-foot demo racquet around Taiwan to sweep Kunnan Inc. into the game.

So I smashed into the real world of racquetball politics.

Politics

---*10*--

Doors open to the stars, and then you run into politics. The best chess and sports masters of every epoch have been closely linked with the values of their societies who pay to watch them. All the flux of a cultural, political, and psychological background is reflected in the game style and strategies of play. The Soviets have chess, and the Americans have rackets.

The rise of the Soviet school of chess to the world summit of board games is their cultural development, and the rise of racquetball was the American form during their 1970's social upheaval, speeded psyches, sexual revolution and the subsequent draw of liberated females by the equipment manufacturers to the sport. The ball makers knew the ladies wanted faster balls and the racket makers pleased them with larger head rackets... that drew more males to the game. In a flash, racquetball became social and successful.

Racquetball politics in the 70s clutch of sex, drugs and rock-and-roll included all night kibitzes with live bands overlooking the Pacific where bartenders mixed girls' cocktails behind the bars with their little pinkies. The racquetball professionals had wealthy seconds, as in chess, and usually at least one lesser player but expert kibitzer as a practice partner. Pro drug abusers were quickly weeded out by attrition from the top eight, but proliferated in the below ranks. Tournament draw sheets wallpapered an entire court lobbies, with three 21-point games sans the tiebreaker. My former housemate, Marty Hogan, to his everlasting credit, was the only player I will never forget who never touched alcohol, drugs and worshiped his grandmother through five world championships.

It takes moral courage to step outside the strategic bell curve, but Hogan did it to become the most influential player in history. As a transplant from St. Louis to San Diego, Hogan wielded an unseeingly deep contact off the navel or rear foot while all the champs hit off their lead foot. Shots blazed off the strings like an errant cannon as Smokin' Hogan turned a deaf ear to a daily smokescreen of ridicule from the snooty champs about his jock size causing his miss-hits. I grew so irritated at the taunts that I threw the Burlington, Vt. pro stop to see him past the finals to better seeding and the top. It wouldn't have been necessary, for the infamous deep strokes became the unbeatable international standard to this day.

It's said that a Soviet diplomat, like a skilled chess or racquet player, does not expect his opposite to give up something for nothing, not even a pawn or point. Yet, in society, this habit may brew trouble. On May 26, 1982, a police patrolman arrested Bobby Fischer as he strolled innocently down a Pasadena sidewalk. The officer said he matched the description of a man who had just committed a bank robbery in the area. The chess star protested, was slightly injured during the arrest, and then was held for two days in jail and subjected to assault and other mistreatments before being released on $1,000 bail.

A decade later, and five miles west of Fischer's seizure, I was arrested by a LA motorcycle officer for jaywalking from a robbery in progress at my own bank! The officer thought my gentle suggestion to glance over his shoulder at the holdup was a bluff, and scratched out a ticket as a cordon of policemen, newsmen and cameramen marched up behind for an interview, as a helicopter zipped overhead. Another officer tapped my arrestor on the shoulder but he was too red faced to tear up the ticket that I wouldn't sign. He cuffed me hard, and shoved me into a patrol car to the LA County jail to languish three days in deplorable conditions. Ether piped through the vents, toilets brimmed with feces, 2000 inmates herded like cattle in an underground vault, concrete floors for chairs and beds, inmate threats under perpetual lights glare, and cigarette smoke everywhere. The three-day seminar would have improved with chessboards instead of bologna sandwiches force fed every eight hours sitting cock-to-butt, before I was daisy-chained with common crooks and bused to court without counsel. The judge who resembled Groucho Marx dismissed the case, with 'Time served'.

Fischer left another legacy on July 13, 2004, acting in response to a letter from US officials when he was arrested by Japanese immigration for allegedly using a revoked US passport while trying to leave the country. Fischer argued that the passport was still valid and was tossed into a windowless cell filled with cigarette smoke for 16 days before being transferred to another facility.

Now I sit in Lake Toba, Sumatra pondering my next chess moves on a bizarre immigration charge of overstaying a visa, which three months ago an embassy official crawled through a window into a locked office for the form that was completed and returned stamped with an incorrect expiration date. My options were to flea via a remote island ferry to Singapore, try to bribe resistant officials, go to the US embassy for help that will alert US immigration to pick me up on return stateside, or a strange variation just presented by the Indonesian immigration chief. He suggests that I enjoy the Lake Toba resort for one more month, until I am legally eligible as a 'criminal' for arrest, and then to jail, immigration court, and deportation. I took that gambit and have used this month to publish two books via print-on-demand from a 24-hour internet with a barking gecko which proves that one not need leave a single room on an outlying island to publish.

Blitz: The Big Game
---------------------------------------*11*---------------------------------------

Blitz chess is also known as fast chess, lightning chess, sudden death, speed chess, and bullet chess. The clocks are set for five minutes each for all of the forty-or-so moves, board life ends in scant minutes, and a fresh one starts. Before mechanical chess clocks were invented in 1883, sandglasses were used at tournaments. The benefits of blitz have always been instant recall of tactics under pressure and an acclimation to adrenalin.

Blitz rackets in tennis, racquetball and paddleball is called the Big Game with a power serve and weak return followed by a put away, often at the tennis net. The racquetball variation is a drive serve, pumpkin return, and killshot. Blitz is the attack style in most modern sports, individual or team, as the strongest strategy of the elite, as sorry as it is to watch.

The sensuous aspect of lightning attack is non-stop concentration for several hours to win before going honkers and, in accord, the national champ is not crazy. Young racket hopefuls of blitz may 'clock' their rallies against practice partners by agreeing that rallies end after the service return to encourage aces and kill returns. The Big Game. That is, there the serve, return, and the ball is picked up by the winner of the abbreviated rally to serve again.

Given one year patient practice in blitz anything, you may win with the pure attack. The evolution of attack in any sport in any player's career generally follows these steps: At the beginner level the defensive player comes out on top by producing fewer errors; and then at the advanced level he falls by the wayside for lacking attack strokes, shots and habit. It's better in almost all sports to begin play aggressively and lose as a beginner in order to have the attacking shots to win as an advanced player. The traditional instruction method that I used as the so-called 'top instructor of racquetball' was to aim first for the bull's-eye, and later add power to the stroke. Now I believe for nearly all sports that an aggressive style is superior from the onset, and in rackets the power stroke should be taught and practiced first before honing on the target.

Physical training for the rackets Big Game is also a new endeavor. Old aerobic plodding marathons and 100-mile bike rides that I did are out; and anaerobic drills such as repeated 30-meter sprints with thirty-second rest intervals are, and repeat for fifteen minutes. Gradually decrease the rest interval and increase the duration to one hour in imitation of modern racket matches. Mike 'The Mighty' Quinn grinned at me once from a whirring Florida treadmill demonstrating the technique, and panting, 'It makes you want to puke!'

Like wild dogs the all-sport blitzers sniff each other on meeting, wrestlers lock eyes at the nude weigh-in, boxers stare down and start slugging, chess players shake hands and sit down to play speed chess, and racquetballers flip a coin before socking the Big Game. The only systems that seem to have defeated blitz in rackets are the squash tin and badminton birdie, and players like me who walked away from the game when it got too fast.

The greatest blitz championship upset was in 1977 at the San Diego Atlas Club locker room where I sat with Davy Bledsoe after losing to him and he counseled by placing his right forefinger on my forehand and crooned, ''My father taught me sports one day by drawing an X on my forehead, and promised, 'You are gifted'.'' That wasn't the greatest upset. It came a few hours later when Bledsoe tore out of the locker room, and raced into the championship court to blitz Marty Hogan with aces and kills to win his sole crown.

Like gold fever, it's very difficult to play against a singles blitz game. You want to go on and on, so an alarm clock should be kept on the side to end the contest in two hours whether it's chess or rackets.

Analysis

------------------------------------ *12* ------------------------------------

My first statistical analysis of racquetball was at the advice of Michigan's regal Paul Lawrence, who enquired, 'Prove to me that the tennis Big Game of serve and put-away exists in racquetball.' He was correct. In recording rally lengths among the nation's top 16 players at an Ann Arbor, Michigan tournament I discovered that the mean rally was 2.3 shots including the serve, return and a little. There was no question that the most important facets of the game were the serve and killshot; they were the *only* strokes. I took that stat to the practice court and many future national titles by won myself and others.

Chess and sport grandmasters find that the most complex unwritten analysis is a one-time opportunity since the mind cannot recreate the conditions and resolve. In studying complicated variations, one often may examine each branch of the tree once and once only. You may see this in the eyes of a certain opponent as he enters the court and glances quickly and once only at you.

Racquetball is sweaty chess, and so the key analysis is physical vs. mental errors. A physical error is a stroke problem that may be corrected via practice; a mental error is poor shot selection that may never be corrected unless pointed out by an aide. Ultimate progress in all sports revolves around separating physical and mental errors, and then fixing them one at a time on a path to perfection.

A day-to-day chart is the best way to improve, and for many years I kept one on my locker door - filling in deficits and corrections - until the daily routine turned into a mental catalog that had no more physical, and only a couple mental errors for a year at a time.

You must have the courage of conviction that if you think your move is good, make it. Nearly all chess players or their seconds in tournaments record chess notations of each game's moves to study later, as football coaches replay videos for the team review. People who want to improve should take mistakes as stepping stones to success, and to accept defeats as the silver linings of goals. Playing without an ongoing critical review gets you nowhere fast, but with it provides a colossal advantage. And once you step off the field, court, or away from the board, analysis charms the mind with a concentration of powers.

Analysis in chess and sport shares these factors:

- It is the main tool of chess in sport.

- Chess helps a child develop logical thinking, decision making, reasoning, and pattern recognition that aid math and verbal skills.

- Chess teaches you that you must sit there calmly and think about whether it's really such a good idea to make a move, and if there are better ideas.

- Analysis is a long-term investment of constant inquiry of the most varied positions to build a store of knowledge in a player's mind enabling him at a glance to assess a position.

- It is not possible to become a great player without learning to analyze deeply and accurately.

I believe not only in chess in sport but in school where I was the Blythe, Ca. SED (Severely Emotionally Dependent, a misnomer) teacher to theoretically defective kids. The first thing I brought to class, and donated another to the school library, was a chess set and board. I told the SED's over the board, 'Chess is such a powerful play in life that if you saturate yourself with the pieces then the game takes you by the hand and points the way.' It worked, too well, some said, and with a few other tricks I worked myself out of a job in one year by 'mainstreaming' all of the students to regular classes, with the gifts of pocket chess sets to proselytize. It was an act in the tradition of Peter Mark Roget who devised the first pocket chess set in 1845, and distributed them with his *Thesaurus.*

Chess and music also go well together. Many historic characters have achieved unusual proficiency in both, such as the 18th century French composer and chess master André Danican Philidor whose *Analyse du jeu des* Échecs was the standard chess manual for at least a century. For five hundred years before Philidor, pawns had less value than in his sway. The best players before him started games with gambits of pawns that were thought of as only small prices to pry open a diagonal file, or to create an intermediate nuisance to a king. But Philidor demonstrated the value of a strong pawn center, and their correct formations, and the relative value of the pieces compared to the rest out the box. He could do prove this in three simultaneously blindfold chess games. It was said that the reason he emphasized the pawns of chess was the political background of 'third rank' citizen pawns of society before the French Revolution started in 1789.

In present day, The Torres Chess and Music Academy believes that every Friday Knight 'It is beyond coincidence that chess and music produce child prodigies with a much greater frequency than that of other intellectual pursuits. While there is no theoretical necessity to explain why this should be so... chess and music ameliorate the rapidly maturing frontal lobe of the child's brain by providing the adequate challenge that it requires to achieve its fullest potential.' For adults, *Chess* is a 1984 musical involving a triad between two top players, an American and Russian during the Cold War, in a world championship, and a woman who manages one and falls in love with the other.

Clock & Scorecard

13

My childhood chess forays against myself were so lonely that one day I devised a three dimensional board with little toothpick men that I thought resembled the world, and felt better. Enter the gamesmen like a clown.

The first racquetball nemesis in more finals that I care to contest was multiple-national champ Charlie Brumfield. His tomfoolery got my best except a few matches, given a fair referee, where I was able to exhaust him until he could no longer utter anything psychologically disturbing. Danish grandmaster Aaron Nimzowitsch said, 'Even the laziest king flees wildly in the face of double check,' and so it is against a gamesman whom you beat their bodies to defeat their minds in winning the day.

One summer I wandered into the Lansing, Mi. King Kone Ice Cream Parlor owned by a 320-pound Ultimate Figurer named Woody who set up a chessboard between milky dribbles. For some reason, there was a hatchet on the wall next to the register where I had paid a buck for a double-dip, but four dips if I won the chess game. Instead of pounding the clock, he smashed the hatchet into the table, wood splinters flying, and he asked, 'What color do you want?' I snatched a pawn from each side of the board in my fists, and replied, 'Left or right?'

That's how you beat a gamesman; ignore his jests. This recalls the great Akiba Rubinstein, who suffered from anthropophobia, a fear of people and society, whose response to 'Who is your opponent tonight?' was, 'Tonight I am playing against the black pieces.'

With the clowns out of the way, the next obstacles are the chess clock and scorecard. They may be ignored, but never beaten until after the next move or shot. These little things tend to bother you in a bad position but not in a good position, and need not bother you at all with a few clock and scorecard twists.

A strong player requires only a few minutes or points in the opening to get to the heart of a conflict. So, the first eight points of a match may be used for a jump start, and to explore the limits of the foe's strokes, service return, shot selection and coverage, and to catalogue them to empower one of two strategies for the remainder of the match. The two strategies are: the weaknesses discovered in the initial points may instantly be 'picked and scratched' to victory, or one may remember them to the end game to tip the scale. Which method to choose depends on the nature of the opponent.

I don't control pace as others try to by playing fast while winning, or vice-versa, except to take a timeout to break a point streak. With an opposer under time or score pressure I discuss general considerations in an internal dialogue, and when I'm under the heat then I analyze specific variations -

each brings prompt focus away from the pressure.

Reverse the score toward the end of a match if you are ahead to avoid losing a won game. Hence, if the score is 8-5 in the tiebreaker to eleven, as the ref intones the score, secretly assign the lower one to yourself. I won two major tournaments without knowing it, and felt stupid left standing alone on the court. A variation is Legend Mike Ray's dissociation from the scorekeeper's call until after match point when he has found himself in the service box crouching to serve as fans flood the court and jump him in congratulations.

Play a won game just as you played earlier with the same neat thoughts, the methodical examination of tactics, but at a quicker rate. Bud Muehleisen calls this turning up the Rheostat 10%. It's a control of play intensity that may also be tuned down in times of crisis.

The strangest things I ever saw in chess was in a Michigan match with 15 seconds left each on my and the opponent's clock, when a west coast girlfriend dropped in for a surprise visit. She opened her arms over the board, and I stood up and moved a piece without glancing from the board, and she stomped out and flew home never to be seen again.

Another time, an odd board set below me as referee in a racquetball California tiebreaker where a player we call Hillbilly paced the court wising his tardy opponent to re-show after a time-out. 'Ref, he's over-due!' cried Hillbilly.

'Idiot,' I retorted, 'Start serving.' The Hillbilly raced for the service box and drive served a short fault. He sprinted to the ball, returned to the box and served a second fault to lose the serve to a ghost. The gallery hooted at the first solo double-fault in history, as Hillbilly stood with hands on hips peering up for one full minute, and then yelled, 'Now forfeit him for not serving in the required time!'

End Game
--------------------------------------*14*--------------------------------------

A working definition of the racquetball end game is the final points, say from a score of 15-15, when the players gulp and eye game point. In a mad rush to 21, adrenalin rains, the ref thunders scores as the fans storm to their feet, and the players throw everything in their gym bag at each other except forgotten combinations. These are the losers at the end game.

On the other hand, champs hold a steady bearing until the last strike of the match. The past – their open and middle games - are prologue to their end games. So it is in chess and all sports. The final moves play themselves out on the platform of the previous stages until the king is tipped or the towel is thrown in.

In chess, a well-played game should be decided in the midgame or even the opening long before the end. In racquetball, it was said as the opponent warmed up that if I tossed my signature racquet cover on the court, I had won in the open. Yet, I always enjoy end games against an opponent who doesn't psych out, because in the end the king becomes the star, a strong piece that one observes in him and oneself between puffs to match point.

The commonalities of chess and sport end games are:

- A study of the classic end games shows the king is brought up as soon as possible even though there seems no particular hurry at the moment; likewise produce your best shots in the first seven points of the tiebreaker.

- Chess world champion Capablanca repeated moves in the end game, often returning to positions on the board which he had had before, to weary his opponent and explore new option; and Muehleisen taught to return to serve and shot options earlier explored and to apply them lethally at the end.

- Chess masters have long trained the body and mind to respond in the difficult final moves.

- A knight ending is really a pawn ending; and in racket sports when the grip is sweaty, body drained and mind failing, the killshot is really a pass.

- The common rook and pawn ending where the rook must be used aggressively matches the racket tiebreaker of fatigue and failure where the killshot must be used without giving quarter.

- The hardest part of chess is winning a won game, however in racquetball one may use the trick of reversing the score to the final point.

- The final moments of strong players are fraught with errors of impatience, complacency, exhaustion, psyching out, or a combination of these.

- If you can move in the end like the open, with confidence and speed, then your matches against otherwise equals are already over.

- There is some validity that after learning the basic strokes, serves and strategies, to forget the rest and spend all the time on the endings.

- Learn the end game by observing a master.

- The last seconds and points are the only aspect of the match that are learned in the crucible.

- The grandmasters had to work hard to achieve strong final moves that appear so effortless to the gallery.

- It often happens that a player is so enamored with his advantage that he is reluctant to put the opponent out of his misery.

- Surprises and miraculous escapes are common.

There are no draws in racquetball… or are there?

No one has played the end game with the grace of world squash champion Victor Niederhoffer who throughout the preface clops about the court never seeming to score while always at least playing even to his opponent. One of the best moves I ever saw on a sports field occurred one midnight session at the Manhattan Racquet Club witnessed only by a nodding janitor whose head jerked up suddenly with the crash of Victor's impact into the front wall on my match point shot. He had vaporized in deep court and reappeared smashed like a bug on the front wall to re-kill and win the serve. When your opponent tenders a draw in chess the rule is to try to work out why he thinks he's worse off. For years I thought he offered the sister's kiss because of injury, but now believe that he wasn't sure if he got the shot before two bounces.

It was my only draw in history, a poor habit since it deprives one the practice of playing the end game.

Beauty of Chess in Sport
15

As the box closes on the pieces after a composition...

One beauty of chess is that it crosses all barriers. Financier George Soros called me Hobo one sunny afternoon at his Southampton home where we split chess games, each winning with white. I discovered he had studied philosophy, and that philosophers quickly adjourn to hermetic strategies across the board.

Chess engraved on the brain doesn't seem to leave. This is especially true after one practices chess in sports during motion. The only flaw of the greatest board game in history is that the board doesn't have feet.

My jogging partner Bob Baldori and I invented aerobic chess on a Michigan track one day with a point man running a few steps ahead wearing a T-shirt magic-marked on the back with a chessboard and pieces in the starting position. This made it easier to visualize the moves as we ran four miles, and the FIDE should silkscreen these shirts for physical fitness.

However, the grandmasters might require silk screened tuxedos for befitting parties. The last one I played against in a speculator's Connecticut home was Arthur Bisguier who with white gave rook odds and gazed between speed moves out the window as if reading a comic book while telling me his life story.

He defeated a young Bobby Fischer and later served as second to Fischer at many international events. He won three US Open Chess Championships (1950, 1956, 1959), and played multiple-game blindfold exhibitions. He was taught chess at the age of four by his father, a mathematician, and kindly never practiced multiplication tables during our match. He thought it terrible, and was pleasantly merciless, that I had disgraced my father while reading funny books in beating him at chess.

After the match, Arthur dropped me off at an Appalachian trailhead near his home, and I took chess onto the trail in hiking the 500-mile Vermont trail, 500-mile Florida trail, 500-mile Colorado trail through the Rockies, the Pacific Crest trail for 1000 miles along the Sierras, the 1000-mile length of Baja, 1000 miles through the Amazon rainforest, and the length of Death Valley. I never would have survived without the lessons from chess.

CHESS AND SPORT

The Search for Bobby Fischer Ends on a Racquetball Court

by Dr. Bud Muehleisen

Here now is my true story regarding Chess in Racquets that I experienced.

Setting: There was a Religious College affiliated with the World Church of God, which was headed at the time by a guy whose last name was Armstrong. They even had a weekly radio show from there. It was a beautiful campus tucked in a three-block square of very expensive property in the wealthiest of districts in Pasadena. It was located between Orange and Colorado Avenues which are the two streets that the Tournament of Roses Parade is held on.

Time: Probably, the late 1970's.

Occasion: They had a beautiful very private Racquetball complex of about three courts and a plush upstairs lounge. I was asked to come up, give a little clinic with their two coaches, play a little doubles with them, and then go to dinner.

Trivia: At the time Bobby Fischer was World Champion and had 'disappeared' (presence unknown) in the World.

Okay, I do my thing and then it is time to play some doubles racquetball. Here's comes the 4th player and they introduce me to Fischer as my partner. He was a total recluse at the time and holed up secretly at the college and had taken up racquetball. He hardly even spoke a word for about three hours and was a C- player.

Anyway, we finish, all go upstairs to the lounge and start drinking tap beer (yes, at the Religious College) and munching on pretzels while watching the Laker playoff game on TV. I noticed two things. There was a gorgeous chess set on the table with the pretzels in between us, and Fischer has a little tiny portable chess set in the front lapel pocket of his coat jacket.

It was quite obvious that he was not there to take part in the conversation, be it racquetball or the Laker game on TV. I ask, 'What's that little portable chess set in your lapel pocket?' He took the time to take the chess set out and matter of factly explain how it was played and utilized. He was reserved, but responded factually and looked me in the eye. Timid is accurate, never bragging while exuding an air of genius. His general continence was what I would imagine sitting across from Albert Einstein who wouldn't need to speak a word for his brilliance to be known.

After a while and idle chatter, there is a knock at the lounge door and it opens,... There stands the LA weatherman with the crazy helicopter swing in Open tournaments. In the those days he did a lot of racquetball promoting in the LA area. In any event, he had arrived late, of course, and missed everything.

So, he sits down and before long he remarks and marvels at the gorgeous chess set between us all on the table. So, I started my 'hustle' conversation with... "Do you play chess, Paul?"... And he replies, "Oh yes, I not only play, but I'm currently the faculty champion at UCLA." I quickly rejoined, "C'mon Paul, I'll bet anyone in this room could beat you... (pause-pause, and then pointing across to Fischer)..... I'll bet that guy right there could beat you, in fact, I'll bet you $50 that he can beat you!"

At the point, Paul looks across at the guy and says in reply..."Dr. Bud, that wouldn't even be fair.... I'm really good!"... I then said..."Well do you want the bet or not?"... He replies.... "O.K., if he doesn't mind?" I look at Fischer and he calmly nods his head in an affirmative gesture. So then I said, slowly and calmly...."O.K. then, (and) Paul let me introduce you to Bobby Fischer."

Now here comes a real classic moment in a confrontation! As Paul stands up and extends his hand across the table to reach for Bobby Fischer's extended hand, who has also stood up by this time... he realizes who he is and before he can utta a word he starts stammering with an "UGGHHH"

Sound drooling out the side of his mouth. He literally could not get out a coherent word from his mouth. It was one of the 'all-time' Hustle's and the rest of us could not stop laughing. Paul slithered back into his seat and was virtually speechless from then on. As he sat there, over the next twenty minutes, he would sneak a peek at Fischer out of the corner of his eye if Fischer was not looking at him. What a moment in time that was.

Of course, Fischer being the non-personality that he was, never said a word the rest of the time either.

After about a 20-minute period of time passed, Paul excused himself to the group saying that he had another appointment. I walked Paul out the door shutting it behind me and when I did... Paul instantly jumped up on my back yelling.... 'How could you do that to me?!!!!'

I don't think I've seen Paul since then and I don't even know of his whereabouts or if he is even alive. I am sure though that he has never forgiven me. True Story.

Moral of the story, and there are possibly many...'Don't ever proclaim any EGO that you might have.....in public'.

So, there is MY story.

PS_BX04430524

CreateSpace
7290 Investment Drive Suite B
North Charleston, SC 29418

Question About Your Order?
Log in to your account at www.createspace.com and "Contact Support."

1/23/2015 05:31:51 PM
Order ID: 81541388

Qty.	Item

IN THIS SHIPMENT

Chess and Sport
1502808625

Racquetball's Best
1505833272

Dr. Bud Muehleisen is the 'father of racquetball' with over 70 national and international championships.

About the Author

Steven Bo Keeley is a Doctor of Veterinary Medicine, former national racquet champion, and has traveled to 105 countries on a shoestring. "My life follows the vicissitudes of Buck the Dog in Jack London's Call of the Wild: From comfortable backyards across America; boxcars on every major railroad; 100+ countries under a backpack; hiking the lengths of Florida, Colorado, Vermont, California, Death Valley, and Baja; to retirement in a desert burrow with Sir the Rattlesnake as a doorkeeper...and a solar computer to write books." In 2007, he became the first California substitute teacher—most requested by students and faculty—to be fired in a playground war. He left to ride the rails with an electronic chessboard, and then became an itinerant expatriate writing from selected global Shangri-Las including San Felipe, Baja, unspoiled Lake Toba, Sumatra, and his favorite since 1999, Iquitos, Peru. His Wikipedia reads like Indiana Jones.

Other Books

Complete Book of Racquetball (1976, DBI Books)

Racquetball Made Easy (1977, Service Press)

It's a Racquet (1978, Service Press)

The Kill & Rekill Gang (1978, Service Press)

Racquetball Flipbook Series (1979, Strokeminder)

The Women's Book of Racquetball (1980, Contemporary)

Hobo Training Manual (1986)

Keeley's Kures (2011, Free Man Pub)

Executive Hobo: Riding the American Dream (2011, Free Man)

Charlie Brumfield: King of Racquetball (2013, Free Man Pub)

Women Racquetball Pioneers (2013, Free Man Pub)

Basic English One Page (2013, Virtual Bookworm)

The Longest Walk (Third Edition, 2013, Free Man Pub)

The Longest Walk Companion (2013, Free Man Pub)

Stories from Iquitos (2014, Service Press)

Advanced Racquetball Made Easy (2014, Service Press)

Greatest Photos Around the World (2014, Service Press)

Chess and Sport (2014, Service Press)

Elvis' Humor: Girls, Guns & Guitars (2015, Service Press)

Bill Schultz: Ringmaster of Sport (2015, Service Press)

CHESS AND SPORT

Made in the USA
Charleston, SC
26 January 2015